IMAGES
of America

DELAWARE STATE POLICE

I0792633

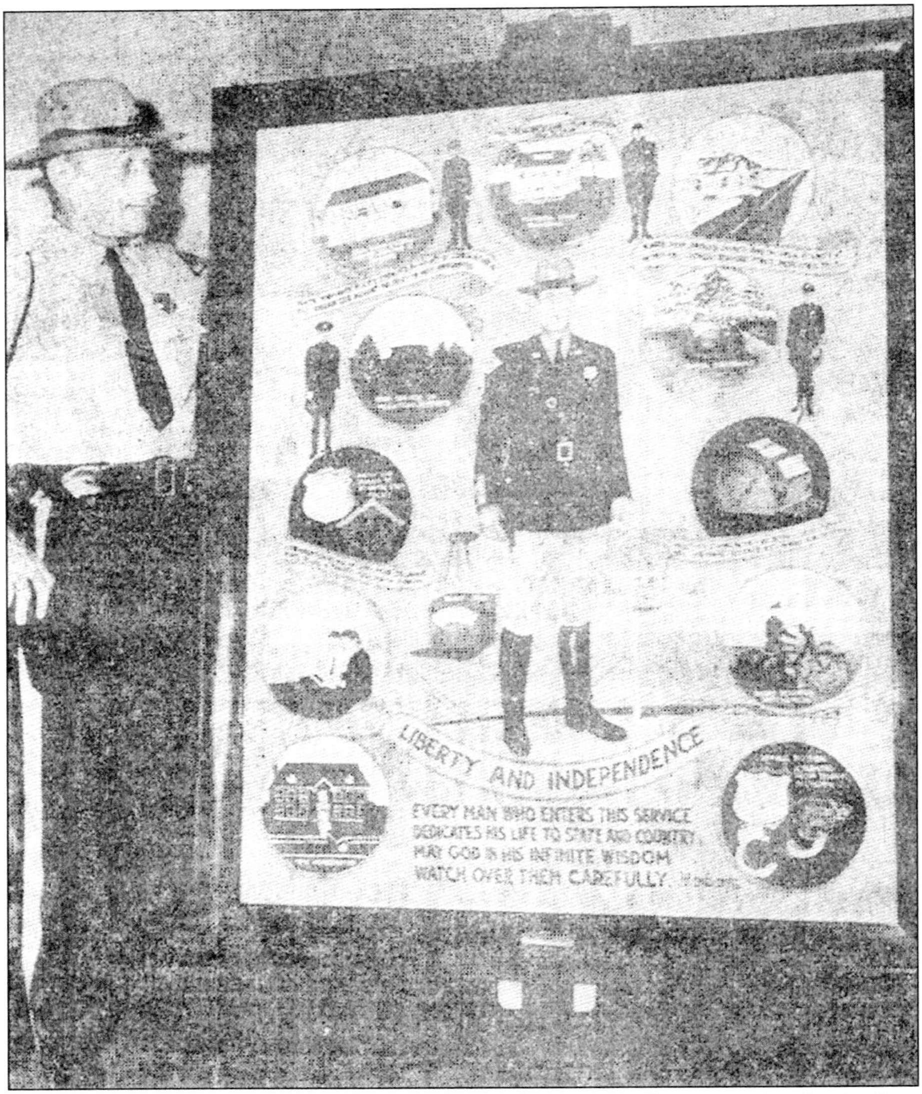

On August 26, 1955, Capt. John F. Herbert Jr., the graphic artist and cartographer for the Delaware State Police, unveiled the first of three murals depicting the early history of the state police force. As chapter headings for Images of America: *Delaware State Police*, portions of this mural have been selected as individual pieces of art. The message on the mural states, "Every man who enters this service dedicates his life to state and country. May God in His Infinite Wisdom watch over them carefully." (Courtesy of the Delaware State Police Museum.)

ON THE COVER: The cover image shows the Delaware State Police force around 1923 on the historic Dover Green on their Harley Davidson patrol vehicles. The man standing in the straw hat is C. Douglas Buck, deputy director of the Delaware Highway Department. His perseverance brought to fruition the formation of this statewide unit. (Courtesy of the Delaware State Police Museum.)

IMAGES
of America

DELAWARE STATE POLICE

John R. Alstadt Jr.

ARCADIA
PUBLISHING

Copyright © 2010 by John R. Alstadt Jr.
ISBN 978-0-7385-8613-7

Published by Arcadia Publishing
Charleston, South Carolina

Printed in the United States of America

Library of Congress Control Number: 2010921460

For all general information, please contact Arcadia Publishing:
Telephone 843-853-2070
Fax 843-853-0044
E-mail sales@arcadiapublishing.com
For customer service and orders:
Toll-Free 1-888-313-2665

Visit us on the Internet at www.arcadiapublishing.com

*To the men and women of the Delaware State Police,
past and present, serving Delaware citizens with
excellent police protection and service since 1920*

Contents

ACKNOWLEDGMENTS

The Delaware State Police Museum would like to acknowledge the many individuals who had the forethought to save the history of the Delaware State Police by collecting a photographic montage of our past and present. The majority of these people are unsung heroes, but several are known to us and include Bernice Biddle, Elisa Vassas, Michael Gunning, and Walter Saxton. We would also like to thank the Delaware State Police and the Delaware State Police Museum Board of Directors for their blessing on this project.

This has indeed been a collective effort, and the author would be remiss if he did not acknowledge the efforts of a small group of research and technical assistants who meticulously searched our photographic archive and assisted in the preparation of this work. A grateful thank you goes to Maj. Robert M. Gouge, Ret.; Capt. Michael E. Neal, Ret.; M. Cpl. Brian C. Anderson, Ret.; M. Cpl. Charles McCall, Ret.; and Elisa A. Vassas, state police photographer. Unless otherwise noted, all photographs are courtesy of the Delaware State Police Museum (DSPM).

INTRODUCTION

At the beginning of the 20th century, there was little need for law enforcement with jurisdictional responsibilities over large geographic areas. For the most part, a county sheriff or city police department could address the enforcement of criminal violations. Given that society's transportation needs were met with horses, boats, or trains, there was no need for traffic enforcement; however, with the invention of the horseless carriage and the rapid growth of that means of transportation, the seeds were sown for the creation of a law enforcement agency to enforce traffic laws over a large territory.

For Delaware, public discussions regarding the creation of a state police force began in 1906. Those discussions centered on a few reports of rural disturbances that either overwhelmed the small town police forces or occurred in areas that did not have an organized police department. But it was the automobile that truly created the need for such a force. In 1911, at the southern end of Delaware, T. Coleman DuPont, using his own funds, began construction of a hard-surface roadway that was to traverse the length of the state. In northern Delaware, there were various turnpikes funded by tolls that were maintained to facilitate transportation in most weather conditions. On the national level, the federal government responded to mounting public pressure for improved roadways by providing funding to the states for highway construction. In 1917, the creation of the Delaware Highway Department, to be overseen by the Highway Commission, began the first organized approach to obtain federal funds for the construction of hard-surfaced roads. And so it was that the growth of automobile ownership in northern Delaware—using, in particular, the Philadelphia "Pike" between Wilmington and the Pennsylvania line—and the reckless driving that ensued caused a public demand for measures to deal with this new menace.

On January 1, 1920, in response to the attorney general's request, the Highway Commission hired Charles J. McGarigle as its first traffic officer. Officer McGarigle was paid a monthly salary of $90 and was provided with a motorcycle for his patrol work. The early success of having a traffic officer patrolling a single stretch of roadway led to calls for additional officers to patrol other roads in Delaware. By the end of 1920, the Delaware Highway Department was employing five traffic officers whose salary, after six months of service, had grown to $125 per month. During the year, six motorcycles with sidecars had been purchased at an average cost of $575 per unit. Also during the year, the Highway Commission authorized the traffic police to use a timekeeper's shack on the Philadelphia Pike as its first station and headquarters.

During 1921 and 1922, the traffic officers continued their duties with no material increase in manpower. A corps of volunteer Citizens' Highway Police supplemented their efforts, but reports of abuse of power by these volunteers led to calls for a state police department. On April 28, 1923, Gov. William D. Denney approved legislation that essentially created the Delaware State Police. On June 11, 1923, eleven men were hired to supplement the existing four traffic officers, and the first organized training class began. Later in the year, contracts were let, and four stations were constructed for the state police—two in New Castle County, one in Kent County, and one in Sussex County.

During the 1920s and 1930s, the motorcycle was the principal vehicle used by the state police for their patrol duties. No man would be hired as an officer if he could not demonstrate that he could operate a motorcycle. Even experienced officers had accidents and spills, and the number of injuries was significant. Several officers suffered injuries serious enough to require amputation of a limb. While the motorcycle was a cost-effective vehicle for patrol work, its utility was limited during periods of inclement weather and was downright dangerous at night on unlit, poorly surfaced roadways. With the cost of automobiles decreasing, the state police were able to purchase enough cars in 1935 to allocate two per troop. But what really turned the tide against motorcycles was communications.

Communication with a trooper while he was on patrol was difficult at best. In the 1920s, a trooper would ride a particular patrol route and stop at the local post office to see if his services were needed. That system was gradually replaced with the telephone. In 1933, troopers were required to telephone their station every half hour and would receive assignments from the desk officer. In 1936, funds were allocated to install a radio transmission system for the state police. This early system allowed for radio broadcasts from the base station to receivers installed in the patrol cars. The receivers were bulky and not weather resistant, thus could not be installed on motorcycles. Over the next eight years, motorcycles were phased out of patrol work in favor of the patrol car.

While the impetus for the creation of the Delaware State Police was the enforcement of traffic laws, criminal violators were not overlooked. The enabling legislation granted troopers the legal classification of peace officers with the duty to enforce state and federal laws. In the early days, whether it was breaking up a gang of chicken thieves or interdicting bootleggers, the troopers gained a reputation for efficient law enforcement throughout the state. An informal practice was developed that had the most senior troopers at each station assigned to conduct criminal investigations as needed. That system was changed in the summer of 1940 when the Investigative Division was created. Each station would have two plainclothes investigators who had the responsibility of investigating criminal complaints and following the cases to their conclusion. This organizational change corresponded with the integration of the State Bureau of Identification, which was the repository for fingerprints and mug shots that had been collected in an organized fashion since the late 1930s. The course was now set to emphasize the scientific detection and collection of physical evidence in support of criminal prosecutions.

In the decades to come, the effort to professionalize police work would increasingly rely upon the adoption of scientific principles. The Delaware State Police were quick to embrace such technology as the chemical analysis of blood alcohol in the prosecution of DUI cases, the use of radar in speed enforcement, and the collection and analysis of trace evidence at crime scenes, leading to the present-day use of DNA for identification purposes. The common thread that binds the early troopers of the 1920s with today's force is the pride of being the best police department that they can be in order to protect and serve the citizens of the state of Delaware.

One

Uniforms and Patches

The uniforms and patches of the Delaware State Police have evolved through the years since the department's inception in 1920 as the Delaware Highway Police. The reader will first be introduced to the Delaware State Police in its infancy and then view its development through the uniforms and patches that officers have worn. A quasi-military organization, the state police has maintained a position of authority through a disciplined uniform appearance.

After years of discussion, dating from 1906, Charles J. McGarigle (at left) was hired on January 1, 1920, as a traffic officer in the newly formed Delaware Highway Police to begin duties relating to the weight, speed, and operation of vehicles on state highways in Delaware. To increase enforcement activities, the Highway Department, which was the parent agency, authorized the hiring of a second officer, Joseph A. McVey (below), on April 15, 1920. They further authorized, during the course of 1920, the hiring of three additional officers to assist in traffic enforcement.

The Delaware Highway Police, later renamed the Delaware State Police, was established by law on April 28, 1923. The first police training school went into session in June of the same year. Under the leadership of Sgt. August Alquist (at right) of the Pennsylvania State Police, who was given the rank of captain, reorganization of the force took place. Training, which was intense, was held in Legislative Hall (the Old State House) for a period of six weeks and included crimes and criminal procedures, motor laws of Delaware, target practice, traffic regulations, and motorcycle instruction. Pictured (below) is the first training class with Supt. Chalmers C. Reynolds.

There have been debates through the years concerning details of the uniform of the first state highway police. Records for this period are almost nonexistent. Research has shown that it was standardized and consisted of one summer and one winter uniform made of wool. Existing photographs show a thigh-length coat, britches, and ankle-cut shoes with leather leggings called "puttees." The summer hat was a standard eight-point design and the winter a leather cap with ears. The winter coat was made of heavy leather in addition to the gloves that protected the hands. The photograph of Joseph McVey (page 10) and these photographs of Edward Carpenter (at left) and John Conrad (below) are a fair representation.

The first uniform generally ascribed to the Delaware State Police dates from 1923; however, a view of earlier uniforms shows a marked similarity. The 1923 uniform consisted of a dark gray whipcord material and was based on the uniform of the Pennsylvania State Police. It had a high military collar with a silver "DEL" on each side. The service revolver was carried on the right side, and officers wore leather puttees to protect their calves. A rounded cap with a peak and a silver hat badge completed the uniform. Officers assigned to Station No. 5, Bridgeville, are shown above in the winter uniform, and Station No. 1, Penny Hill, officers sport the summer uniform at the Wilmington train station below.

The first uniform was not well received by the men, as it was somewhat cumbersome for wearing on a motorcycle. In addition, though the high collar offered protection from the elements, it was uncomfortable on the neck and tended to cause chafing after an extended period of wear. Pvt. Harry A. Pusey (at left) models a variation of the uniform, and Pvt. Owen Hession (below) and a second officer model individual variations of the uniform outside a justice of the peace court in Wilmington.

Though retaining some of the style, including the britches, puttees, and the "flying wheel" patch, the Delaware State Police introduced a second uniform. The second uniform was instituted on May 17, 1925, and was altered only slightly. The greatest change was the blouse, which was fashioned after the one worn by the New York State Police. Rather than the high military collar, the new uniform had a roll collar and a tie. The holster with a Sam Browne belt (shoulder belt) was moved from the right side to a cross draw. Pvt. George E. Minner (at right) and Pvts. John Conrad, Walter White, and Clarence Buffington (below) are in the uniform with and without the patch.

As the Delaware State Police entered the decade of the 1930s, changes in the uniform were afoot. In 1931, the General Assembly authorized a new uniform that consisted of, for winter, a navy blue whipcord blouse with olive tabs on the sleeve, olive drab britches with a blue stripe, black shoes, puttees, and a gun belt with cross-draw holster. The summer uniform had the same britches and foot material, but the shirt was a navy serge material. The hat was eight points made of navy-colored whipcord. Pvt. George W. McConnell (at left) is seated dressed in the winter uniform. Pvts. Wilbur Bush, Edward C. Beswick, and William A. Leach (below) relax in the summer uniform.

A second significant event took place on March 1, 1932, under the auspices of the Highway Commission, which authorized an addition of a new shoulder patch. Worn on the left shoulder, the new insignia became known as the "hen and chicks" patch. The emblem was embroidered by hand, and the story of its origin can be traced to a little old lady in Wilmington who labored on each so that no two were exactly alike. Fact or fiction, it is a good tale. From left to right Pvts. Clarence K. Lynch, Harry A. Pusey, and William H. Horney are shown at right outside Station No. 4, Georgetown. Station No. 3 privates are shown (below) standing inspection at the Old Sesquicentennial Building in Dover.

The United States's entrance into World War II brought about changes within the Delaware State Police. Due to the war effort, there was a shortage in material resulting from the conversion of garment manufacturers from peacetime to wartime. A new summer uniform was adopted in 1942. Khaki in color, it was identical to that issued to the military. Uniform additions were a blue serge stripe on the pants, a black tie, and a blue cap. In cooler weather, a lightweight field jacket was issued. Troopers attending a fingerprinting school at Dover (above) are wearing the new uniform. Trooper Richard R. Smith's photograph (at left) shows the second version of the "hen and chicks" patch.

In an attempt to modernize the Delaware State Police, a new uniform based on the style worn by the New York State Police was introduced in 1944. The cross-draw holster was abandoned in favor of one worn on the right side. The blouse was dark blue with light blue trim. Each shoulder of the blouse and shirts had "Delaware State Police" in gold letters on a gold diamond, the department's fourth patch. The shirt and britches were a light blue for winter and a dark blue for summer. A Sam Browne belt, knee-high boots, and a Stetson hat completed the uniform. Over the years, from 1944 to 1956, the Stetson would share the stage with a more traditional eight-point hat. The photograph above is the class of November 1946 in the winter uniform with Supt. Paul Haviland (right) and training director Harry Shew (left). Troopers William Carson and Horace Willey (at right) are shown in the summer uniform.

Officially the Delaware State Police deserted the Stetson hat in favor of the eight-pointed hat in August 1947, when Col. Herbert Barnes became superintendent. However, as late as 1959, it appears that the Stetson was still in use by the division. In that year, another major change occurred with the introduction of the fifth patch of the Delaware State Police. It was designed by Capt. John Herbert and is a seven-color patch based on the Great Seal of the State of Delaware. Shown at left are Troopers Ernest Spence (left) and Irvin Smith (right) in the winter uniform with Stetson hats around 1956. Trooper Walter Saxton (below) is shown in the summer uniform of the same period.

The present uniform has changed little since the introduction of the style based on the New York State Police in 1944. The two greatest changes were the transition from the Stetson hat to the campaign hat, which is based on the hat of the Pennsylvania State Police and is dark blue in color, and the movement away from the traditional boots and britches. Cited as a cost factor, today's trooper is issued straight-leg pants and black shoes with boots and britches as optional, should the trooper desire to incur the expense. Trooper William Thorpe (right) and Trooper James Mood (left) are shown in a hat transition photograph at right. Trooper William Skibicki (below) is shown in the dress uniform of the Delaware State Police around 1973.

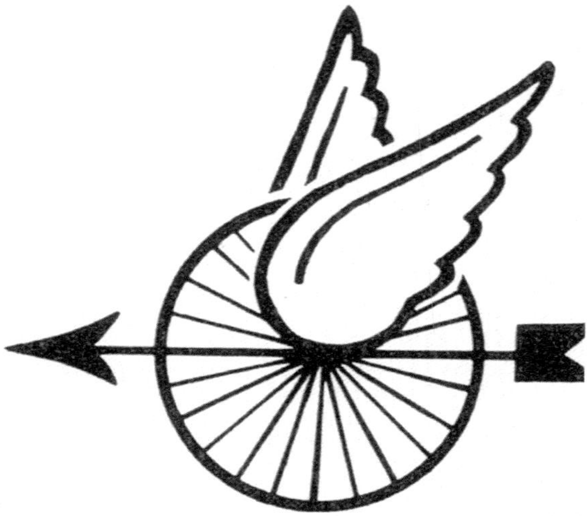

The first shoulder patch adopted by the Delaware State Police appeared on officers' uniforms in the early 1920s. Known as the "flying wheel," it denoted the motorcycle era of a number of state police agencies in the United States. The second shoulder patch of the Delaware State Police was the "hen and chicks" patch. Adopted in March 1, 1932, the patch depicts the state of Delaware and its three counties within a diamond, as Delaware is known as the "Diamond State."

The third patch of the Delaware State Police was adopted around 1942 and is an adaptation of the second patch. Also known as the "hen and chicks" patch, the only difference is the enclosing of "state police" within the diamond. The fourth patch, referred to as the "Diamond Patch," was adopted on May 4, 1944. It was worn on both shoulders and has "Delaware State Police" in blue lettering on a gold diamond. It stems from Thomas Jefferson's statement that Delaware, because of its location, was the "diamond" of all states on the East Coast.

The present patch of the Delaware State Police was adopted in June 1956 and put into service on a new uniform, which was authorized at the same time. The patch is a seven-color depiction of the Great Seal of the State of Delaware. The state seal was adopted on January 17, 1777, and contains the state's coat of arms. Descriptions of the seal are as follows: the wheat sheaf was adapted from the Sussex County seal and signifies the agricultural vitality of Delaware; the ship is a symbol of the New Castle County shipbuilding industry and Delaware's extensive coastal commerce; the corn is taken from the Kent County seal and also symbolizes the agricultural basis of Delaware's economy; the farmer with hoe represents the central role of farming to the state; the militiaman with musket recognizes the crucial role of the citizen-soldier to the maintenance of American liberties; the ox represents the importance of animal husbandry to the state economy; the water stands for the Delaware River, the mainstay of the state's commerce and transportation; and the motto was derived from the Order of Cincinnati and approved in 1847.

Two

BUILDINGS

When highway police officers were hired, no thought was given as to what facilities should be provided. Late in 1920, the Highway Commission realized that the officers needed shelter from inclement weather. They authorized the use of existing timekeeper's shacks on the Philadelphia and Kennett Pikes. There is no record concerning the Kennett Pike station, but the Philadelphia Pike station became the first headquarters.

From 1920 through 1923, this timekeeper's shack (above) served as the headquarters and first patrol station for the Delaware Highway Police. On April 28, 1923, legislation was signed into law expanding the Delaware Highway Police force and effectively creating the Delaware State Police. In conjunction with that expansion, funds were allocated to construct five stations throughout the state. Station No. 1, as shown below, replaced the timekeeper's shack. This station was believed to have been located on the Philadelphia Pike north of Delmore Place.

The photograph above clearly shows the proximity of Station No. 1 to the southbound shoulder of the Philadelphia Pike. Contrary to the building that it replaced, this station did not function as a headquarters. For a short period of time, headquarters remained at Bellevue Hollow until rented office space was obtained in the city of Wilmington.

In 1927, as the force continued to expand, $4,000 was appropriated for the purchase of a suitable site for the construction of a new Station No. 1. This site is on the southwest corner of the Philadelphia Pike and Washington Street Extension. This brick building (above) is complete with a detached garage for servicing motorcycles.

During the 1930s, Station No. 1 (above) became the site for the first Teletype machine, which linked police agencies in eight states. Also during this period, the State Bureau of Identification was established at Station No. 1, and the need to store fingerprint records necessitated an expansion of the building.

In the late 1950s, Station No. 1, now known as Troop 1, had simply outgrown the building. As shown above, additional office space was added through the use of a trailer, which housed the detective division.

A larger Troop 1 was constructed behind the existing troop, and upon completion of the new troop, the former troop (above) was demolished with the exception of the weigh scales. The new building, which is still in use today, included a firing range in the basement and a detached full-service garage located in the rear.

With the expansion of the force in 1923, there was a need for additional stations in other parts of the state. Station No. 2 (above) was established in the vicinity of State Road, which is the convergence of U.S. Route 40 and U.S. Route 13. This station was constructed on the northbound shoulder of the highway and was used for less than five years. (Courtesy of Delaware Public Archives.)

In the mid-1920s, it was decided to expand portions of the DuPont Highway (U.S. Route 13) into a dual highway. The original Station No. 2 was in the right-of-way for the new northbound lanes and had to be replaced. In 1928, a new Station No. 2 (above), constructed of stucco, was built on the southbound shoulder of the highway, roughly across the road from the original station. The original 20-ton weigh scales were replaced with 30-ton weigh scales.

As was the case with Station No. 1, the second Station No. 2 (above) quickly became too small to serve its purpose, and the building was expanded. Note that on the near side of the building, an exterior stairway was used to access the basement, which housed utilities and storage.

On September 23, 1950, the state police opened their latest Troop 2, located just north of the intersection of U.S. Route 40 and U.S. Route 13. Situated in the median, the large glass wall afforded a view of what was then one of the more important intersections in Delaware. The unusual design of this building was the basis for its nickname as the "ferryboat." The photograph below shows the view from the roof in the rear of the building looking north with the combined U.S. Routes 40 and 13 on either side. This is a typical troop inspection conducted in the early 1950s. Note that a detached full-service garage is located on the far end of the property.

As a part of the original construction of stations in 1923, Station No. 3 (at left) was built on the DuPont Highway, near the intersection of Leipsic Road. Originally budgeted at a cost of $674, the station was completed in February 1924 at a final cost of $864.25. The second Station No. 3 (shown below) was originally constructed in Philadelphia for the sesquicentennial exposition in 1926. A businessman purchased the building and had it disassembled and reconstructed on the DuPont Highway north of Dover. It had a rather short life as an inn, and after it was vacated it was purchased for use as Station No. 3 as well as the Kent County office for the state highway department. This building served as Troop 3 from 1935 until the completion of the new headquarters in 1958, when Troop 3 was combined into the front portion of that new building.

The actual location of the second Troop 3 can be determined from this aerial photograph. The complex of buildings located to the left of the troop (north side) is a garage/trucking business with a small airport facility in the rear. That property was subsequently developed to become the present-day site of Dover Downs Raceway.

During the summer of 1923 what became known as Station No. 4 (above) was constructed on the DuPont Highway, north of Georgetown. At this early date, no weigh scales had yet been installed at the various stations. The highway was made of concrete and was 14 feet wide—insufficient in width to allow two vehicles to pass each other without using the shoulder.

In the photograph above, Station No. 4 is shown in the early 1930s with the addition of a set of weigh scales visible under the motorcycles. While the principal vehicle used in patrol work was the motorcycle, a sidecar was occasionally used, and each station had a car assigned to it for use on midnight patrols. During the late 1930s, a new brick station (below) was constructed for Georgetown. Note that the building behind this station is the former station building that is now being utilized as a maintenance facility for the station's motorcycles. (Above, courtesy of Delaware Public Archives.)

This aerial photograph (above) shows the unique placement of the second Station No. 4. It is bordered on the right by the DuPont Highway, U.S. Route 113, and on the left by North Bedford Street, which leads into the town of Georgetown. In the lower photograph, taken in 1958, this same building is now known as Troop 4. The structure has doubled in size with an addition on the north side (front) of the building, and the original station, which had been used as a garage, has been removed and a new vehicle maintenance building has been constructed.

In June 1925, a temporary Station No. 5 was located at the Seaford Bridge. In July 1925, this permanent Station No. 5 (above) was opened north of Bridgeville, approximately 1 mile south of Greenwood. At the time of its construction, 20-ton weigh scales were being installed at the various stations. In 1938, Public Works Administration funds were obtained to construct this new Station No. 5. The site of this troop (below) was on the northbound shoulder of U.S. Route 13 and on the inside of a slight curve. Its proximity to the highway proved hazardous over the years, as it was struck several times by errant motor vehicles.

As early as 1925, plans were discussed regarding the construction of a troop on the Kirkwood Highway between Wilmington and Newark. Through the years, there were repeated requests made to fulfill that original plan, but action would not be taken until May 18, 1964, when the above structure was purchased by the state and opened as Troop 2-A. In 1969, this troop's designation was changed to Troop 6, and in February 1971, a new 8,000-square-foot facility, as shown below, was opened. As seen in the background of this photograph, the troop was located adjacent to the New Castle County Workhouse (prison).

Providing sufficient manpower to patrol the resort area in southern Delaware was an issue that dated to the 1940s. Troop 4 in Georgetown was responsible for this territory and would assign extra troopers during the summer months. In 1957, a small residence was converted into a substation of Troop 4 and designated Troop 4-A. At the dedication ceremony, Capt. George Tidwell (above, right) and Highway Commission member Robert Thompson raised the flag. This substation was manned 16 hours per day, only during the summer. By 1970, it was upgraded to Troop 7 and was staffed year-round.

In November 1963, a squad of six troopers was assigned from Troop 2 to patrol the newly opened Delaware Turnpike. Five years later, the manpower would be increased to 13, and what would become Troop 8 was established in a trailer near the turnpike administration building. The troop was later incorporated within the administration building, but by the end of 1976, the troop was decommissioned and patrolling of the interstate highway system was assigned to Troop 6.

On May 26, 1969, Troop 2-A in Odessa (above) was opened in a converted state highway department garage. This building was the scene of a shooting of an off-duty trooper on August 24, 1970, when Carl Henry fired a shotgun through the front window of the building, striking Trooper Dewey Evans in the back. Trooper Evans was hospitalized and eventually recovered from his wounds. The troop would subsequently become Troop 9 and, on February 19, 1972, would be replaced with the three-story brick structure pictured below. The facility, at a cost of $484,527, was large enough to house 23 troopers as well as the State Police Auto Theft Unit.

During the 1920s and 1930s, headquarters were located in rented offices in the Lodge Building on King Street in Wilmington. In 1939, the structure (above) was constructed to house headquarters, Station No. 2, and offices for the Highway Department. Within nine months, this building proved too small, and Station No. 2 was relocated to its prior building on the southbound shoulder of the DuPont Highway. This structure also served as a training facility with a classroom on the first floor (shown below, Lt. Edgar Isaacs is instructing an accident investigation class). In 1958, a new headquarters complex was constructed just north of Dover, and this building became the fourth Troop 2.

On July 17, 1957, a cornerstone ceremony was conducted at the new state police headquarters building on the DuPont Highway, north of Dover. The front of this building would house Troop 3, while the rest of it would contain the executive staff and support services, the State Bureau of Identification, and the traffic section. A full-service garage complex, which also temporarily housed the training academy, was erected in the rear of the main building. The aerial photograph below shows the configuration of the complex as well as a vacant plot to the left of the main building, which would be the site of the new training academy in 1970.

In 1956, this structure was converted from a construction building into a training academy. It was located on the north side of the approach roadway to the Delaware Memorial Bridge. The small building nearest the camera was the firing range officer's observation point. In the below photograph, taken in the opposite direction, the firing range as well as the single span of the Memorial Bridge are visible. This facility was used until 1959, when the training academy was moved into a building located behind the new headquarters in Dover. Although not a factor in closing this facility, construction began in 1964 on the second span of the Delaware Memorial Bridges, and this site became the approach to that second bridge.

After closing the training academy at the Memorial Bridge approach in 1959, it would be 11 years before the state police would have a fully functioning, stand-alone structure dedicated to training police officers. In March 1970, at a cost of $604,000, the building pictured above was dedicated and welcomed its first recruit class. The academy consisted of a second-floor dormitory, while the first floor housed two classrooms, offices, and an attached multipurpose gymnasium. Pictured below is Capt. James L. Ford instructing the 35th state police recruit class in early 1973. Note the audio-visual equipment, which was considered state of the art in its day.

In February 1948, the Delaware Association of Chiefs of Police (DACP) announced its decision to construct and operate a summer youth camp near Assawoman Bay. Maj. Herbert Barnes spearheaded this project and enlisted the volunteer efforts of many troopers in the construction of the camp. In recognition of the efforts of Colonel Barnes, the camp was later named in his honor. The free camp can host up to 60 children for one-week sessions during the summer months. In the below photograph, Colonel Barnes (in uniform) is seen displaying the project plans to members of the DACP.

Three

VEHICLES

Motor vehicles in our history cannot be understated. Initially, the most efficient means of transportation was the motorcycle. There were efforts to make automobiles available. Private autos were loaned to the department, followed by the purchase of one per station. Transition from motorcycles began in the mid-1930s. By the early 1940s, motorcycles were no longer the primary vehicle. Since the 1950s, the department has employed a wide variety of patrol and specialized vehicles.

By the end of 1920, the Delaware Highway Department had purchased six motorcycles with sidecars at an average cost of $550 per unit. Pvt. Earl Cole is shown standing next to his motorcycle with sidecar attached in this photograph taken on the Philadelphia Pike in the early 1920s. Note the "foul weather" windshield attachment to the handlebars. In the mid-1920s photograph below, from left to right, officers Freeman Messick, Claude Beswick, Charles Knox, Henry Ray, Owen Hession, and Horace Ritter are seen standing next to their respective motorcycles in front of Station No. 1 on the Philadelphia Pike. While sidecars increased the stability of motorcycles, they were not routinely used on patrol, as they severely limited maneuverability.

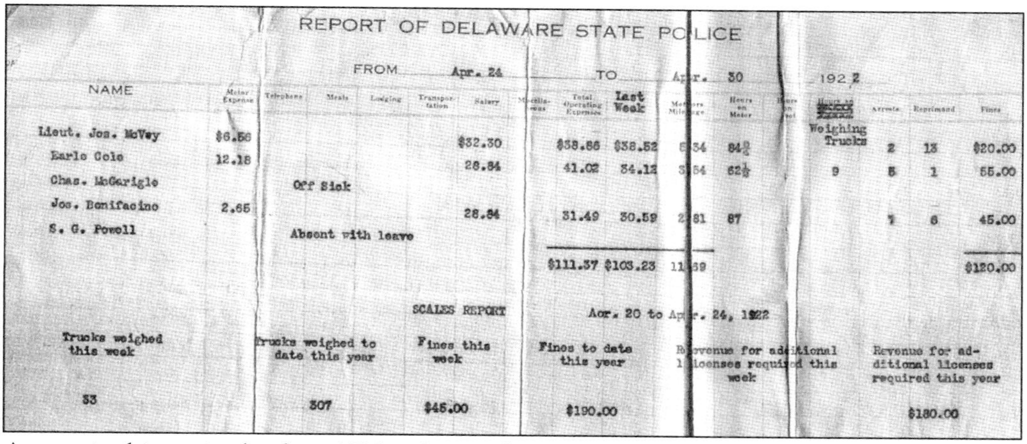

REPORT OF DELAWARE STATE POLICE

FROM Apr. 24 TO Apr. 30 1922

NAME	Motor Expense	Telephone	Meals	Lodging	Transportation	Salary	Miscellaneous	Total Operating Expenses	Last Week	Motors Mileage	Hours on Motor	Hours on Foot	Hours Weighing Trucks	Arrests	Reprimand	Fines
Lieut. Jos. McVey	$6.56					$32.30		$38.86	$38.52	5 34	84		Weighing Trucks	2	13	$20.00
Earle Cole	12.18					28.84		41.02	34.12	3 54	62½		9	5	1	55.00
Chas. McGarigle		Off Sick														
Jos. Bonifacino	2.65					28.84		31.49	30.59	2 81	87			7	6	45.00
S. G. Powell		Absent with leave														
								$111.37	$103.23	11 59						$120.00

SCALES REPORT Aor. 20 to Apr. 24, 1922

Trucks weighed this week	Trucks weighed to date this year	Fines this week	Fines to date this year	Revenue for additional licenses required this week	Revenue for additional licenses required this year
53	307	$45.00	$190.00		$180.00

As seen in this station log from 1922, police work was very different from the present day. Privates worked 60 to 80 hours per week for an annual salary of $1,500. Only three of the available five officers were working that week, and they logged over 1,100 miles on their motorcycles.

What may have been the entire fleet of patrol cycles in seen here in front of Delaware Cycle Company, located at 840 French Street in Wilmington. In 1926, the fleet was switched from Harley Davidson to Indian Cycles, but by 1927, the fleet was converted back to Harley Davidson.

By the 1930s, motorcycles were getting larger with more powerful engines. Here Pvt. Horace Hickman is seen with his cycle in front of Station No. 4 in Georgetown. Although the cycles were becoming more sophisticated, note that they still lacked a windshield.

Motorcycles continued to increase both in size and motor power. Here is a late 1930s patrol cycle parked in front of headquarters on the DuPont Highway. This shows one of the earliest installations of a radio on a motorcycle. During this era, the radios were only capable of receiving one-way base transmissions. By the late 1940s, the transition to radios eventually led to the phaseout of motorcycles for the Delaware State Police.

Motorcycles were first revived in the 1970s with a trial program using two units for patrol of the Interstate Highway System. Cpls. Charles Bethard (left) and Arthur McGee are seen in front of Troop 1 with their new Harley Davidson motorcycles. This program was later discontinued due to safety and utility concerns.

While most patrol work in the 1920s utilized the motorcycle, there were occasions when an automobile would be used. Often these sedans would be loaned to the patrol force, and as such, they were not marked, nor did they have lights or sirens. Pvt. Henry Ray is pictured here with one such auto.

In 1935, the first patrol cars were purchased—one for each station. By 1938, the force had a total of 25 patrol cars and 33 motorcycles. Pvt. John W. Blizzard is photographed at Station No. 4 beside a 1938 Ford with its unique markings and siren/emergency light.

While an unusual vehicle for a police department by present-day standards, this late-1930s Ford Woody was most likely used as a staff car or for the transportation of evidence equipment to crime scenes throughout the state, and thus would have been an early evidence detection vehicle. Pictured are Det. Francis Callahan (left) and Det. Wilbur Bush.

The patrol cars used during World War II were a mixture, given that no passenger cars were produced for civilian use. Pictured here are 1941 marked and unmarked patrol cars as well as a safety education vehicle parked behind Station No. 4.

As World War II was drawing to a close, civilian auto production increased, and the state police were able to add 1946 Fords to the fleet. This photograph shows the varicus pieces of emergency equipment that were carried in the trunk of a patrol car during that time.

This photograph of a 1949 Ford patrol car shows the convertible stretcher assembly that was carried in the trunk. In rural areas, the wait for an ambulance might be significant, thus the ability to convert a patrol car to carry a critically injured person to the hospital was very important. This concept was adapted years later with the acquisition of the first helicopter. In the below photograph is the special shelving that was installed in the trunk of these patrol cars in order to properly store the stretcher assembly.

The Delaware State Police were featured in a July 1960 article in *Popular Science* magazine that examined the growing trend toward unmarked patrol cars. At one time, Delaware's fleet of cars was 100 percent unmarked. In addition to Fords and Chevrolets, the fleet consisted of Plymouths and Nash Ramblers. Pictured from left to right are Col. John Ferguson, J. Gordon Smith (chairman of the Highway Commission), and Maj. Sterling Simonds accepting delivery of a Nash Rambler.

Trooper Donald Beebe is pictured with a 1958 marked Chevrolet patrol vehicle. This vehicle was unique in that it was the first vehicle in the 1950s to utilize a roof light and fender lighting. Although unmarked patrol cars were favored during this time, there was a need for a marked car for escort and parade purposes.

Trooper Donald Beebe is shown again with a 1958 Ford in a semi-marked condition. The absence of roof lights was still a safety concern, however. There was also a need to show police presence at an accident or crime scene, and having a distinctively marked vehicle served that purpose.

In 1958, two Dodge patrol cars with push-button transmission controls were loaned to the state police for six months. These vehicles were to be driven around-the-clock in general patrol service and then returned to the manufacturer to be analyzed for durability. Pictured here is one of the vehicles with its operator, Trooper First Class Dwight Boyce.

In November 1960, the state police embarked on a publicity campaign to emphasize the enforcement of speed limits. This Plymouth patrol car was enhanced with a roof-mounted speedometer so that motorists could determine the accuracy of their own speedometers while following this car. Gov. Elbert Carvel (center) and Col. John Ferguson (far left) are shown with government dignitaries.

An example of the unmarked patrol cars in use during the early 1960s are these two vehicles parked on the shoulder of Kirkwood Highway, near the building that was to become Troop 2-A and eventually Troop 6. The car on the left is a 1960 Ford, and the right car is a 1962 Plymouth.

By the 1960s, the state police began the transition from 100 percent unmarked patrol cars to an eventual ratio that favored marked cars. Seen above is a 1963 Chevrolet patrolling the JFK Memorial Turnpike at the Delaware-Maryland state line.

With the acquisition of its first helicopter in 1971, the state police moved to increase coordination of search operations by marking the roof of patrol vehicles with their car numbers. Here Thomas Logullo applies the numbers to a patrol car while helicopter HQ 501 pilot Charles Nabb observes.

In the early 1970s, a federal program to target drunk drivers began. Known as the Alcohol Safety Action Program (ASAP), it featured distinctively marked patrol cars that were dedicated to late-night patrols seeking drunk drivers. Shown above is a 1972 Plymouth used in that program.

In 1974, in response to the nationwide speed limit enforcement effort, the state police implemented a Tactical Accident Control (TAC) unit that utilized specially marked 1974 Plymouth patrol cars. The TAC units would conduct saturation patrols on the major roadways, targeting speed limit violators.

During the 1970s, the Plymouth patrol car dominated the state police fleet. The 1973 model Plymouth (center in the above photograph of a Troop 6 inspection) was a particular favorite with its 383-cubic-inch, 8-cylinder engine.

During the 1980s, Chrysler Corporation continued to dominate the police patrol vehicle market with its Dodge Diplomat. Shown above is a typical marked Diplomat from the mid-1980s. While most patrol vehicles were rotated out of routine patrol work when they logged 100,000 miles, it was not unusual for these vehicles to still be in non-patrol service with over 150,000 miles.

In January 1946, the state police acquired a GMC 2.5-ton truck from government surplus. This vehicle was reconstructed and outfitted for use as a mobile field unit. It was supplied with a full arsenal of weapons and riot control equipment as well as two electrical generators and four floodlights. A complete public address system was also installed, and the unit carried portable stretchers and a 14-foot-by-14-foot hospital field tent. In the photograph at right, Capt. Samuel Stant (right rear) is shown briefing other officers on the equipment and its capabilities.

Unfortunately, the chassis of the 1946 unit proved to be too cumbersome for field use, and in 1948 the body was removed and placed onto a Ford F-8 chassis with cab. Note that this latest unit was equipped with a portable radio transmission tower stored on the roof. The photograph below shows an officer demonstrating the public address system.

In 1960, when it was decided that the necessary repairs and upgrades to the existing field unit would be too costly, this replacement vehicle was acquired. The vehicle pictured above incorporated an expanded communications capability to more properly manage a police operation.

In 1965, the state police acquired, from federal surplus, a weasel for use in patrolling off-terrain areas such as beaches and swamplands. The vehicle is seen here making its public debut in the area of Legislative Hall in Dover.

In 1974, the state police converted a 1971 Volkswagen Beetle into a safety education vehicle. Known as "Trooper Dan," the car was equipped with its own campaign hat, a red light for a nose, and eyeballs on the windshield wipers. This vehicle would be used in conjunction with school programs, and a trooper would converse with students through a hidden speaker in the front of the vehicle. Trooper Dan would acknowledge students by shifting his eyes or flashing his nose. Pictured below is the rear of Trooper Dan displaying his "aviation markings."

In the early 1960s, the state police acquired this trailer and equipped it with a variety of displays in order to promote safety education. The trailer would be towed to various events as well as the state fair and would be staffed with officers from the Safety Education Unit.

One of the more unusual vehicles acquired by the state police was this airboat. This boat allowed access to most inland waterways and bodies of water, particularly the marshland areas, for the purpose of search and rescue.

In 1975, funding was obtained for the purchase of three crime scene vans. These Criminalistics Units were fully equipped to be self-sustaining at a crime scene through the use of an onboard generator and lighting equipment. In addition to what had become standard tools, such as photography and fingerprint dusting kits, these vans were equipped with enhanced capabilities to recover fingerprints from difficult surfaces, specialized lighting to detect body fluids, and ballistic evidence recovery such as gun powder residue.

With the proliferation of highways that effectively bypassed the troops equipped with weigh scales, the need to weigh trucks with portable scales became important. The Truck Enforcement Team acquired this van with a trailer for hauling portable scales to remote locations.

Four

Traffic Safety

The 20th century introduced the "horseless carriage." Motor vehicles were a danger, as operators disregarded the safety of others. Dirt roads were replaced with paved highways, which allowed speeds of 35 miles per hour, thus traffic safety was a primary concern. The highway police were tasked with curbing rogue drivers, enforcing vehicle laws, and weighing overloaded trucks. The state police has expanded its traffic safety duties in a number of areas related to motor vehicles.

Through the years since its inception, the Delaware State Police has attempted to grab the attention of the public through a variety of messages relating to traffic safety. In later years, the messages have become sterner than they were in the division's early years, but then it must be remembered that those were much simpler times. Though the thoughts were simplistic, the message (at left) was clear. Pvt. John Derrickson (below) was one of an increasing number of officers of the Delaware Highway Police whose acquaintance offending drivers would meet. Their style was unique, as evidenced by the shiny object in the top of his left boot. In the precomputer age, the officer used a paper punch to put a hole in the driver's license. Different offenses had certain locations on the license, thereby allowing the officer to note how many violations the driver had incurred.

The majority of citizens in the state of Delaware, as well as visitors, are familiar with a traffic safety tool used by the Delaware State Police to assist officers in performing their patrol function. Instituted around 1968, Operation Road Check (above) allows troopers to set up checkpoints and stop all drivers. A simple request is then made for the operators' license, registration, and insurance card. Compliance allows the operator to only suffer a short delay in his travels. Little known is the fact that Operator Road Check actually had its roots in 1925, as evidenced by Pvt. Daniel Sullivan (below) and a fellow officer.

An unfortunate consequence of the motor vehicle has been the incidence of accidents on the highway. Though not initially trained to cope with accident investigation, the Delaware Highway Police, and subsequently the Delaware State Police, took the initiative in responding to property, personal injury, and fatal crashes. What, at first, appears to be a morbid sense of humor (at left) is, in reality, a poignant message to the motor vehicle public regarding traffic safety. This message depicts the grave consequences of disregarding traffic rules, as does the photograph of Pvt. Edward Carpenter (below) painting an "X" on the DuPont Highway at the scene of a fatal accident.

The advent of large vehicle traffic on highways designed to carry the general public brought about its own inherent risks, which are no different than the hazards of our age. Paramount in the minds of the officers working then, as well as now, was to cope with the traumatic aftermath of operators of vehicles involved in deadly and near-deadly collisions. Pvt. Daniel Sullivan is shown above in 1926 on the DuPont Highway in Dover investigating an accident involving a truck and a car that resulted in a fatality. Pictured below is Cpl. Arthur McGee on Interstate 95 beginning the investigation of a dump truck accident in 1976.

Throughout the years, the Delaware State Police has continued to devise ways of honing its skills at curbing the ever-present danger of motor vehicle collisions. The effort has included better educating the officers whose responsibility it is to determine the cause and remedy the situation. The group above is seen at Legislative Mall receiving a demonstration of how to determine the speed of a vehicle from skid marks left prior to a collision. The poster at left of the newly created Charting and Drawing Division, drawn by Cpl. John Herbert, a theatrical artist and art designer, was used as a cartoon-type accident prevention media. (Other posters by Corporal Herbert are included on pages 66 and 68.)

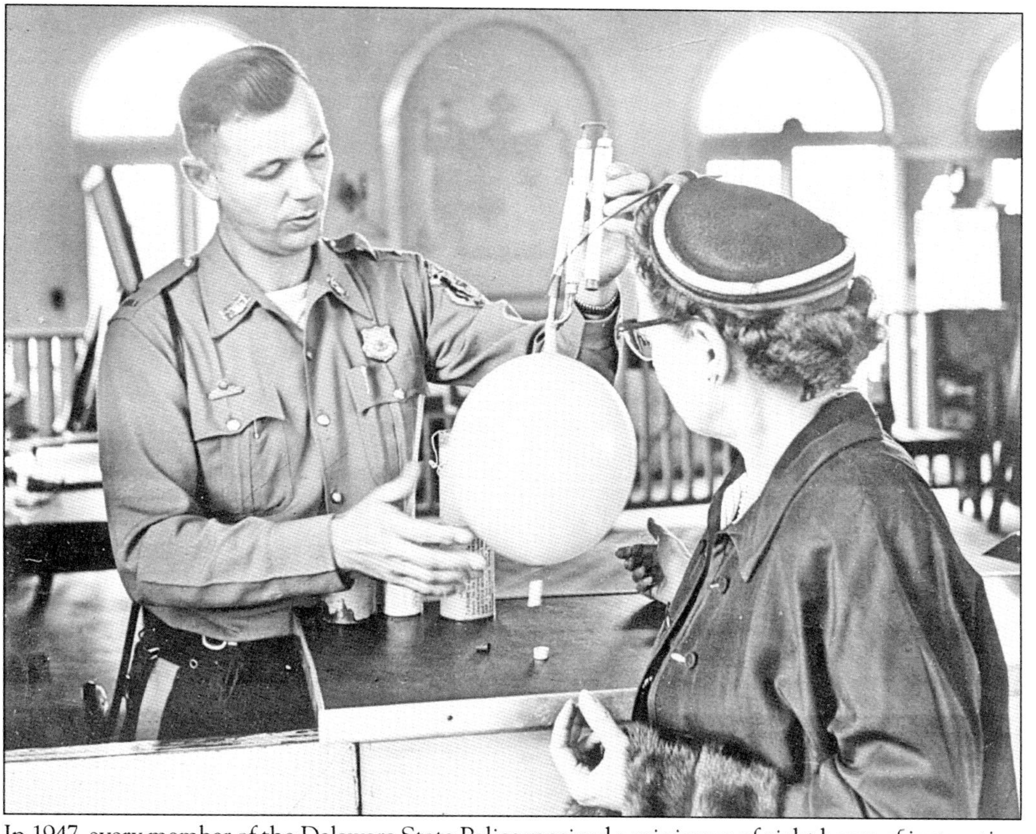

In 1947, every member of the Delaware State Police received a minimum of eight hours of instruction in the use of the Intoximeter, a chemical test to determine the degree of alcohol in a person's blood by means of an analysis of the breath. The device was developed by Dr. Glenn C. Forrester and is being demonstrated above by Trooper Horace Willey. The test was first introduced to the public on New Year's Eve 1948. As the test evolved through the years, its name was changed to Mobile Operation Breath and Alcohol Test (MOBAT). Trooper Walter Saxton is shown below administering the test to a subject at Troop 3 in the late 1960s.

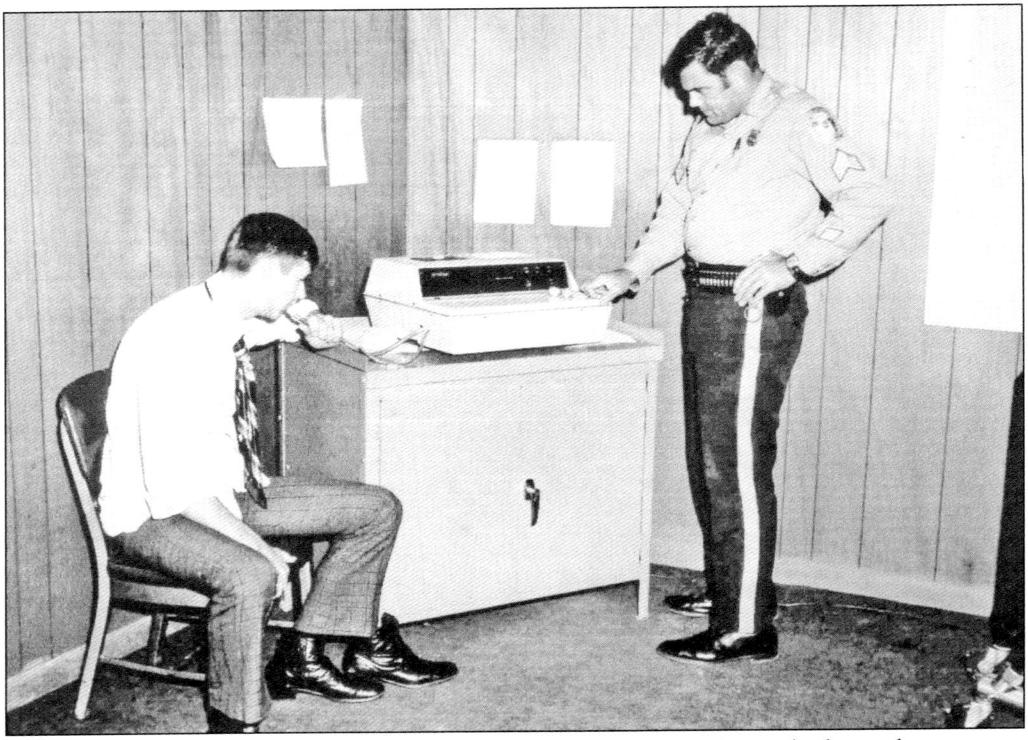

Having had initial success in reducing alcohol-related motor vehicle incidents from 1947 to 1974 through the use of the early balloon-type devices, the Delaware State Police introduced a new instrument in 1975—the Omicron. As demonstrated by Sgt. William Carter of Troop 3 (above), it was mechanical in nature and gave instant results to the operator through a machine-generated printout. The Omicron machine of the late 1970s is still in use today, though later generations use the name Intoxilyzer. Also implemented by the Delaware State Police in the 1970s were sobriety checkpoints (at left), which were similar to Operation Road Check, but for the specific purpose of apprehending drunken drivers.

Throughout its history, the Delaware State Police has had novel and innovative means to educate the public on the dangers of operating a motor vehicle while under the influence of intoxicating beverages. In addition to chemical tests, poster campaigns, and road checks, the officers at various troops have sought the use of visual aids to inform drivers of the consequences of drunk driving. At Troop 1, Penny Hill, (above) a jail cell was erected adjacent to the Philadelphia Pike in 1959. Trooper First Class Leroy O'Neal points to drivers and to the message which states, "YOU . . . Stop and Think – Don't Drive and Drink." A more modern message from the early 1970s at Troop 2, State Road, (at right) was much more graphic and went directly to the point. The tombstone states, "If Drinking and Driving Is A Must Then Drink Your Fill & RIDE WITH US."

The mandate that created the Delaware State Highway Police appears in chapter 213, volume 30 of the Delaware Laws, April 2, 1919, and states that representatives (officers) shall have the right to stop all vehicles exceeding the prescribed limits of the law and weigh such vehicles, provided it shall not delay such vehicle more than 30 minutes. Pictured above are vehicles stopped at the weigh station at Troop 3, Dover, complying with the law in 1924–1925. These early weighing procedures, it was found, served a secondary purpose: they afforded officers assisted by agricultural inspectors the opportunity to inspect the vehicles' cargo for contaminated produce and poultry (below).

Through the years, the Delaware State Police has maintained a portion of its selective enforcement unit for the express purpose of weighing large vehicles. As the stations of the 1920s became obsolete and new troops were built throughout the state, new weigh stations were incorporated into the facilities to accommodate larger and heavier vehicles. The photograph above shows Sgt. Herbert Barnes at Troop 2, State Road, inspecting a driver's license while weighing a tractor-trailer in 1939. Weigh stations continued to be an integral part of the troops landscape into the late 1960s, as evidenced by the trooper below weighing a large vehicle at state police headquarters in Dover. Gradually phased out, the permanent facilities were replaced by a weigh-in-motion operation in the 1970s and 1980s.

As an innovative tool of police agencies throughout the world, the video camera mounted on the windshield of police vehicles to record all evidence of what was occurring during a traffic stop was thought to be a product of the computer age. The Delaware State Police, as early as the late 1930s, was apparently using an early innovation of this tool on at least one patrol vehicle. Cpl. William Knecht, Troop 1, Penny Hill, is shown above standing outside his patrol vehicle with its roof-mounted camera and fender-mounted speedometer. Pictured below is a camera's-eye view of a vehicle proceeding northbound along the DuPont Highway at a recorded speed of 70 miles per hour.

In February 1952, the Delaware State Police implemented a new device for traffic safety with the expressed intention of curbing reckless and speeding drivers on the highways. It was a stringent step to halt the rapid rise in highway fatalities in the state. Using radar (above) for the first time, the apparatus, which was borrowed from the Highway Department, was put into operation on U.S. Route 13 northbound at Tybout's Corner. The use of radar and unmarked cars was met by stiff resistance and caused an immediate political controversy. Sgt. Allen Fields (left) and Trooper John Ferguson are pictured below setting up a radar point after its general acceptance as a highway safety tool.

As controversial as the use of radar as a traffic safety tool was in 1952, it has become generally accepted as a motor vehicle enforcement device through the years. Large and cumbersome when first initiated, the units have become continually smaller and more mobile since their inception. Pictured above is a trooper in the late 1960s operating radar on a secondary road in Sussex County. Initially used by radar teams, the later devices, due to their mobility, can be operated in a variety of ways. Trooper First Class Ward Gagnon, Troop 6 patrol unit, is shown at left setting up a radar checkpoint in 1973 with a catch vehicle, barely visible in the distance.

The Delaware State Police has performed a variety of traffic safety duties throughout its history. Most citizens are familiar with the major roles undertaken by the division pertaining to speed enforcement and related offenses, accident investigation, and drunk driving, but are less familiar with some of the secondary functions. In the late 1940s, Trooper Burrill McCoy is pictured above as a crossing guard at a local school in Kent County. Today traffic lights are considered the norm by society, but in the early 1950s, they were not so commonplace. Trooper George Scholz is shown at right setting up precautionary devices on Maryland Avenue. These devices were once carried in patrol vehicles to assist officers in facilitating the movement of traffic.

Sgt. Clarence K. Lynch began to organize a driver education program in Delaware during 1939, but the war years curtailed the program until 1943, when preinduction driver education courses began statewide. Sponsored jointly by the Delaware State Police, the Delaware Safety Council, and State Department of Public Instruction, the course received national recognition when magazine articles were published in 1946 and 1947 in *Women's Home Companion* and *Redbook*. Lynch is shown above at Milford High School awarding certificates to two students in 1939. The photograph below shows Lynch (now a lieutenant) instructing a student in proper parking techniques around 1949. Assisted by five driving instructors, Clarence Lynch supervised safety education and drivers' education at Delaware's 23 high schools.

Five

Criminal Investigations

The highway police were authorized to perform traffic-related duties. This vision was carried forth when the state highway police began on April 28, 1923. It was recognized that the force should not be confined to traffic duties, but should be given the authority to enforce all Delaware laws. Officers began a dual function of both traffic duties and criminal investigative responsibilities. This was the case until mid-1940, when the Criminal Investigative Unit was established.

The 18th Amendment, which brought about the days of Prohibition, found the Delaware State Police thrust into a new area of law enforcement. Assisted by Federal Prohibition, the officers became quite adroit at ferreting out illegal liquor stills in the rural parts of the state of Delaware. The photograph above shows, from left to right, Pvts. Norman Voshell, unidentified federal agent, Oscar James, W. D. Lank, and Joseph Holt at a still in a wooded area in Sussex County. The still, which was allegedly owned by a Brian Lynch, played a significant role in his murder trial in February 1924. In the photograph below, Pvts. Raymond Ingram (left) and Oscar James (far right) are assisted by a federal officer at a another still in a Sussex County cornfield.

In March 1925, Pvts. Charles Knox (left) and Owen Hession, while on patrol in the Station No. 1 area, exhibited the value of having a statewide police force by apprehending Luther and Andrew Bevins at Naamans, Delaware. The two brothers were fleeing north following the shooting of two Maryland State Police officers who were transporting them from Snow Hill to Baltimore on unrelated charges. Following their capture, the brothers were taken to the Wilmington police headquarters and photographed with their captors. Pictured below from left to right are Private Knox, Snow Hill sheriff Purnell, an unidentified Maryland trooper, Luther and Andrew, an unidentified U.S. Marshal, Private Hession, and state police superintendent C. C. Reynolds. (Courtesy of *Every Evening Journal.*)

FARMER SLAIN; $3100 IS STOLEN, KILLER CAUGHT

James Baker, Youth, Kills 78-year-old James A. Carey, Whaleysville Farmer, With Club—Captured by Delaware State Policemen With Girl Companion Who Has Some of Money in Stocking

On July 17, 1925, the Delaware State Highway Police once again showed its worth as a statewide police force. As reported in the *Every Evening Journal* on July 18, 1925, (above) a farmer, James A. Carey, was slain during a robbery in Whaleysville. Ten minutes after being notified of the crime and the perpetrator James Baker's involvement, he was captured by Pvts. Edward Carpenter (below, left) and David R. Zeigler (right) at his home near Selbyville, Delaware, with the stolen currency.

In January 1926, Harry Butler of Sussex County was arrested by the Delaware State Highway Police for the rape and assault of a young girl in the Georgetown area. A mob (above) gathered at his arraignment on February 9, 1926, at the Georgetown courthouse and surged against a barbwire fence, which had been set up for security purposes. Despite their best efforts, officers were forced to call upon the National Guard for assistance, who employed tear gas to disperse the crowd. Butler was taken from the jail by the state officers, who were pursued by carloads of angry rioters, and safely housed in the New Castle County Jail. Butler was returned to Georgetown at the time of his trial and, following his conviction, was hanged (at right) as a crowd of hundreds watched.

Delaware has a large and vibrant poultry industry dating back to its founding in the 17th century. The "blue hen chicken" (above) accompanied Delaware regiments during the American Revolution and the Civil War. Poultry stealing during the Great Depression became a major problem for farmers in Kent and Sussex Counties, and a special night patrol of state policemen was initiated in 1933. These patrols, plus the use of signage (at left) on farmers' barns and poultry houses, proved to be a successful deterrent. (Above, courtesy of Elisa A. Vassas; at left, courtesy of Capt. James Spicer, Ret.)

On March 27, 1935, the Delaware State Police was authorized by the state legislature to purchase fingerprinting equipment. In July 1935, Sgt. William Knecht (at right) was charged with the responsibility of establishing the State Bureau of Identification. He transformed a jail cell at Station No. 1, Penny Hill, into a work area for acquiring fingerprints from arrestees and a repository for fingerprint cards. This original program has evolved into the use of computer-enhanced fingerprints and an automated defendant photographic system. Pictured below are Maria Lyons (left) and Virginia Pavey conducting data entry on the first generation of the Automated Fingerprint Identification System.

Fingerprints as an investigative tool used to identify criminals have a very storied past that dates from the beginning of the 20th century. The procedure for collecting a person's individual impressions has changed little through the years. Pictured at left is believed to be Pvt. Charles Shockley collecting rolled impressions from a subject in the 1930s. Collecting impressions is only the first step in the procedure, and Lt. William Knecht (below) is shown conducting an in-service training class for fingerprint classification in 1940.

Police identification photographs, commonly referred to as mug shots, have been a part of the investigative process since the invention of the camera. With the establishment of the Identification Division in 1935, the Delaware State Police cast about for a more advanced technique. In 1940, following the creation of the Criminal Division, Lt. William Knecht (above) began using a large-format camera to place photographs along with fingerprints in the state police identification files. By the 1970s, a more streamlined process was adopted with the introduction of Polaroid cameras. Cpl. Rolf Wysock (below) demonstrates this photographic advancement, which made photographing subjects much easier.

The use of scientific methods in the processing of crime scenes during the 1940s is illustrated above by Det. John Joseph, who is shown conducting a preliminary blood test on a piece of evidence collected during an investigation. Much the same as the techniques used by the fictional Sherlock Holmes, crime scene processing has grown in stature during the years.

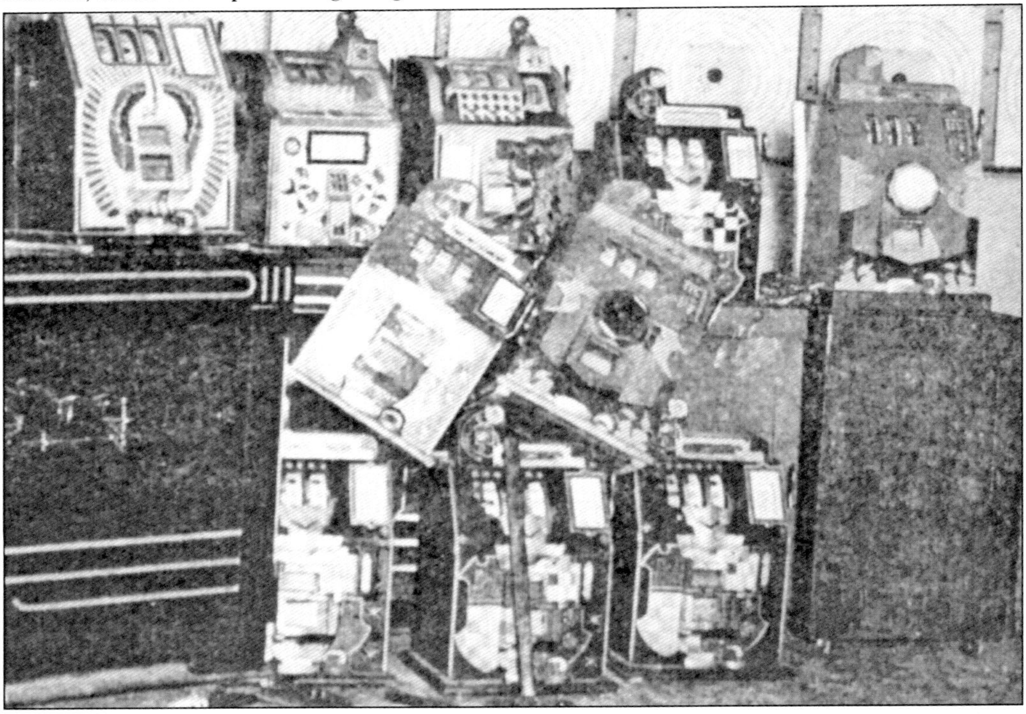

Criminal investigation covers a wide spectrum of events. This photograph depicts one of those venues—illegal gambling. In July 1945, the Delaware State Police conducted a raid on the Peoples Bank Building in Middletown, Delaware, and seized 37 one-armed bandits and destroyed several gaming tables.

The use of innovative crime-fighting methods has been a hallmark of the Delaware State Police since its inception. In January 1952, the Criminal Division acquired a World War II surplus mine detector, which was used to recover buried metallic stolen property. Det. Eden Jones (left) and Det. Joseph Eckrich (right) demonstrate this tool. A second innovation used to fight crime came into use in 1965. This was the "Identi-Kit," which consisted of hundreds of sketches of facial features. Det. Robert Forenski (below) demonstrates the technique used to construct a composite picture of a suspect.

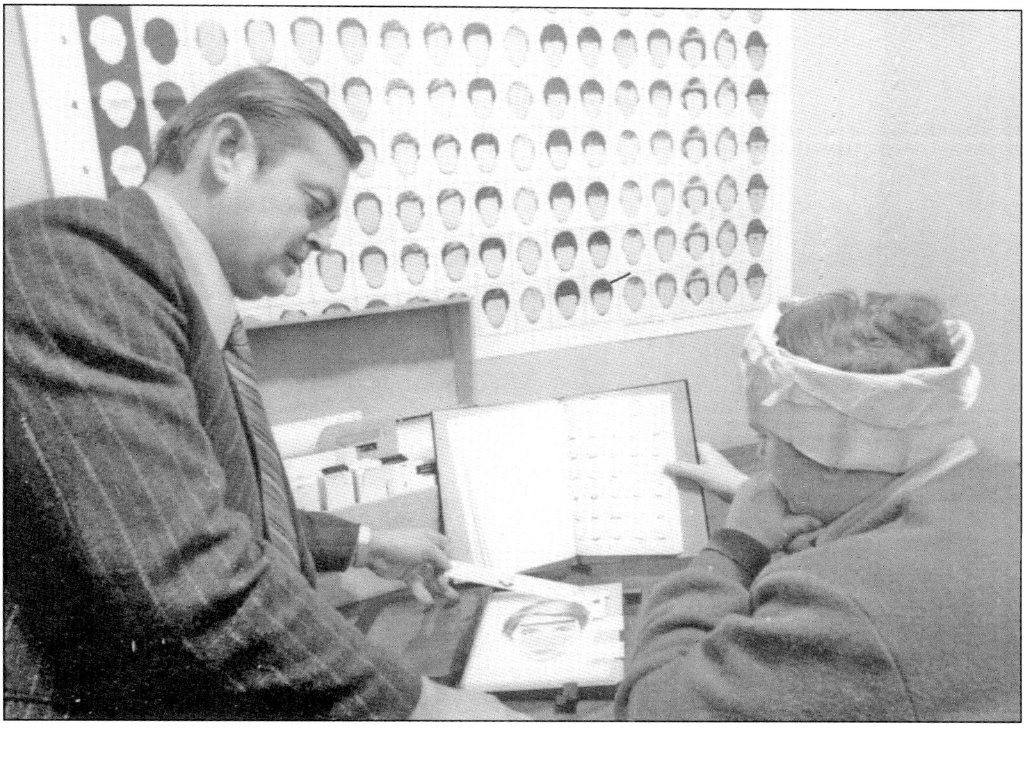

The photograph at left is a portion of an actual crime scene that occurred on November 4, 1943, in Rehoboth Beach, Delaware. John Worthington, a U.S. Army warrant officer, was murdered by coworker Carl "Frenchie" Moulinie, who was having a love affair with Elaine Worthington, John's wife. Dubbed a "Death in the Lakeside Home," a miniature crime scene was created by Capt. Sterling Simond (below, left) and Sgt. John Herbert (below, right) in 1952. Based on the Francis Glessner Lee "Nutshell" training concept used by the Harvard Homicide School, this miniature scene was used as a training tool for the Delaware State Police. It is now a permanent display at the Delaware State Police Museum, where young and old alike can test their crime-fighting skills.

From its inception in 1940, the Criminal Investigative Unit saw relatively quiet times within the state. Minor criminal activity occurred, but major crimes were not the norm. There was the "Lakeside Murder," but nothing of the magnitude that took place in 1948 and 1949. In those years, perhaps the most gruesome murders of the decade took place and were dubbed "The Lonely Hearts Murders." Perpetrated by Inez Brennan and her son Bobby, the crime gained national prominence. Pictured in the photograph above is Inez Brennan, who is flanked by Det. Joshua Bennett (left) and Capt. Melvin Leisure (right) in the Kent County Courthouse in Dover, Delaware.

Recalling the Butler case of 1926, the year 1952 saw a crime nearly as heinous in Kent County. Alex Church (wearing baseball hat) and James Blevins (front center), flanked by Det. Charles Hughes (far left), Det. Maurice Fitzharris (second from right), and Capt. Aubrey Reed (far right), are escorted from their arraignment for the violent rape of a female child. They were subsequently found guilty and incarcerated at the New Castle County Prison.

The murder of Martin Luther King Jr. on April 4, 1968, sparked some of the worst riots in the history of the United States. Delaware, and specifically the city of Wilmington, was not spared during this civil unrest. On April 8–9, 1968, rioting commenced, and the Delaware State Police was ordered by Gov. Charles Terry to mobilize and respond to assist the Wilmington Police Department, along with the National Guard. Pictured at left are four-man units of state troopers and guardsmen who patrolled the streets attempting to stem arson, looting, assaults, and curfew violations. Snipers were prevalent during this time, and Sgt. Peter Steil (front, center), Cpl. Frank Klair (behind Steil and to his left facing the camera), Trooper Andy Roth (farthest right), and two unidentified troopers are shown at left scanning adjacent buildings for activity.

Through the years, crime scene investigation has become more specialized, and the Delaware State Police has remained at the forefront. During 1975, the division created a new unit within the Criminal Division whose responsibility entailed the collection of evidence at crime scenes. This unit was known as the Criminalistics Unit, and later the Evidence Detection Unit. Three specially equipped vans were outfitted with the latest crime-fighting technology. Pictured at right is Det./Crpl. John Alstadt demonstrating on-site latent fingerprint processing, which is but one aspect of the unit's capability. Another aspect of the unit is the collection and preservation of physical evidence. Detective Alstadt (far left), Det. James Dillon (center), and Det. George Patterson are shown below removing body parts from an explosion at Getty Oil Delaware City on March 20, 1978. (At right, courtesy of Bonnie Waller, *Delaware State News*; below, courtesy of Dan Miller, *Delaware Today*.)

Combating the sale of illegal drugs has always been a challenge for law enforcement. Educating the public in the identification and the consequences of illegal drug use is but one tactic. This premise was put to use by the Delaware State Police in the 1940s. The photograph above shows a display of illegal drugs and their street names. The photograph below, which was taken in the early 1970s, shows the continuing effort as Lt. Thomas Littel gives a lecture to a group of students inside the State Police Community Service trailer.

Six

Specialized Units

From its inception, the state police has strived to remain at the forefront in law enforcement, being proactive rather than reactive as a police agency charged with the public trust. The state police has created areas of specialization to assist in the performance of its duties through the years. The following pages will give a sampling of these innovative techniques, which have enhanced the functionality of the department.

The Delaware State Police was tasked in early 1930 with the responsibility of regulating the fledgling air traffic industry. Its duties included the inspection of all planes and the licenses of all pilots flying in the state of Delaware. This photograph was taken at Bellanca Airfield in New Castle County, Delaware, and includes the inspecting officers Supt. C. C. Reynolds (second row, third from left) and Guiseppe Bellanca (far right) of the Bellanca Aircraft Company.

In 1955, the Delaware State Police embarked upon a new venture in the field of aviation with the creation of the Aviation Section. Beginning initially with a rented aircraft, the department began patrolling the skies as a means of curbing speeders with "flying traffic control." Pictured here is Sgt. Charles Skinner, who is believed to have been the Delaware State Police's first pilot.

The first air-to-ground traffic arrest in Delaware occurred in 1955. The photograph at right shows pilot Lt. William Short and his traffic observer (unidentified) preparing for a traffic enforcement mission. Having used rented planes since its inception, the Aviation Section acquired its first permanent aircraft, a Cessna 175 Skylark, on June 21, 1960.

On February 18, 1971, the Delaware State Police ventured into a new age of flight with the acquisition of its first helicopter, a Bell Jet Ranger. Pictured are Lt. James Ford in the foreground and, from left to right, Capt. Walter Nedwick (Ret.); Col. Gerald Lamb (Ret.); Gov. Russell Peterson; Fred Vetter, public safety; and Col. George Bundek accepting delivery of HQ 501.

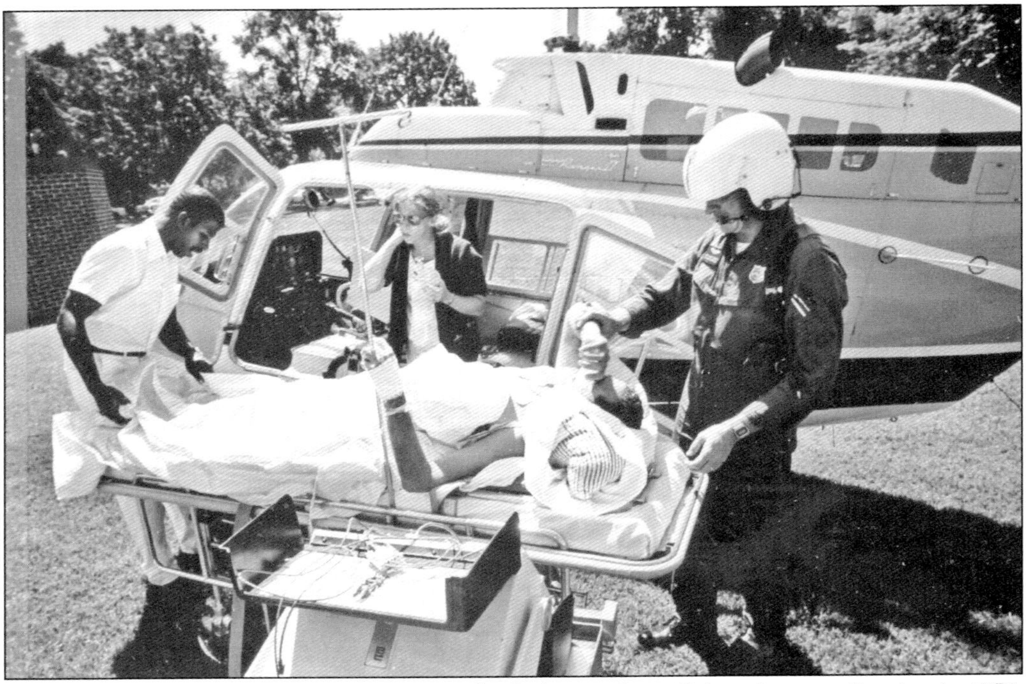

Since its introduction as a separate unit in the Delaware State Police Aviation Section in 1971, the helicopter's role has changed dramatically. Its original mission was for search and rescue and to assist troopers with criminal air searches. The role quickly changed when, with the addition of a medical technician (above), it became an airborne ambulance. Aviation's primary mission has not changed significantly, but with the addition of certified trooper medics, it has become a lifesaver. The helicopter now has the capability of whisking an injured person to hospitals throughout the state in less than 20 minutes. Aviation also performs a secondary role today by rapidly deploying special operations officers, members of the scuba unit, and the K-9 unit. The photograph below depicts the helicopter in one of its additional roles of transporting K-9 assistance to a crime scene search.

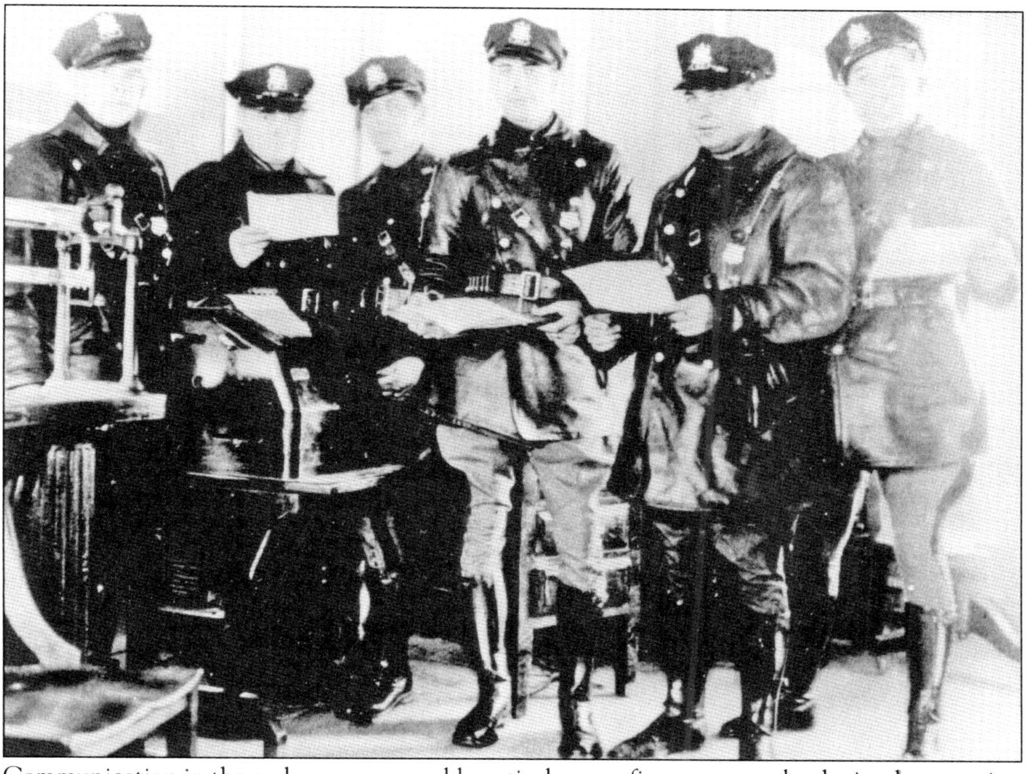

Communication in the early years was problematic, but was first overcome by the implementation of a flag system in 1925. Locations of buildings equipped with these flags were published in the local newspapers, and citizens in need of a police officer would go to an identified location and display a red flag for the next passing officer. Simple at best, it did offer citizens a venue for relief. Communication between police agencies was overcome in November 1934 with the implementation of a Teletype system, which connected Station No. 1 to other nearby states and assisted with apprehension of fugitives. Officers J. Cole, G. McConnell, T. Plummer, R. Carpenter, and two unidentified are pictured above from left to right.

A second innovation occurred on August 5, 1936, which was the installation of one-way radio transmitting equipment at stations throughout the state. This allowed the transmission of radio messages to patrol officers who had receivers on their motorcycles. Unfortunately it was only a one-way transmission, and officers still had to stop at stores and request the location of their response. Cpl. Herbert Barnes is pictured operating an early radio transmitter at Station No. 2.

While war is generally viewed as a tragic event, it also brings about advances in technology, and World War II was no exception. The results of this global conflict brought two major advances in communications: a more advanced Teletype system and the introduction of the two-way radio communication system. Pictured above is Cpl. Hugh Harrity at headquarters, State Road, operating an advanced Teletype machine. From this point onward, advancements in communications continued unabated. The 1960s and the 1970s saw greatly improved communications equipment with the implementation of communication centers in each county as well as a main center in Dover, Delaware. Communications specialist Frank Sparks is pictured at left in the Dover Center in the 1970s.

Firearms proficiency, due to the nature of police work, has always been a hallmark of the Delaware State Police since its inception. No records exist prior to 1938 as to the location of firearms training, but one need only use a little imagination to come to a conclusion. It is a fact that, with the completion of the new headquarters at State Road, the facility was equipped with the indoor range pictured above in the basement. The first identified outdoor firing range was used in the late 1930s and was located at the "Sandpits" behind the Farnhurst Hospital in New Castle, Delaware. Pictured below are officers qualifying with their service revolvers. Pictured below, Cpl. George K. Shockley and Pvt. William Davidson clean their weapons after qualification.

The first formal firing range developed by the Delaware State Police (above) saw its advent in 1953 during the construction of the Delaware Memorial Bridge on property owned by the State of Delaware. A state-of-the-art firing range for its time period, it was used for a number of years for qualification of both recruits (below) and sworn officers. Incorporated into this property in 1956 was the first formal recruit training facility, the original Delaware State Police Academy.

A common belief is that the Delaware State Police's K-9 (canine unit) traces its origins to 1958, and in the general sense, this is true. However, the true origin occurred in 1925 when Francis V. DuPont, a friend of the state police, purchased four German shepherds on a trip to Europe. Upon his return, he donated the dogs for use as guards at the four state police stations. Pvt. Daniel Sullivan is pictured going for a ride with the station's canine, Judy, and her pup, Ike. (Courtesy of the *Wilmington Sunday Star.*)

Interesting stories aside, the formal organization of the Delaware State Police K-9 Unit occurred in September 1958. The initial K-9 unit consisted of three dogs trained for crowd control and criminal searches of both terrain and buildings. Pictured above are Trooper James Ford with his German shepherd Chinook and Trooper Joseph Rowan with King, a Belgian shepherd.

Trooper First Class Thomas E. Everett, with his partner Captain, a Doberman pinscher, was placed in command of the first K-9 unit by Col. John Ferguson and his staff. Early training took place at the Dover Air Force Base and at Macy's in New York City. Originally comprised of three men, a fourth—Trooper Harold Rupert with his German shepherd Rocky—was later added. Early successes included numerous fugitive apprehensions and maintaining the peace in Collins Park during the Rayfield Bombing case in 1958.

Due to the early successes of this initial unit, the Delaware State Police K-9 Unit has continued to expand since its foundation. The role of the unit has continued to change over the years as well as expand in size. Used initially to search for humans, the canines have been used through the years to search for drugs and explosives. Pictured above is the unit in the early 1970s and includes, from left to right, Troopers E. Wharton, W. Bergstrom, T. Inman, E. Heston, R. Kocher, E. Morris, R. Pierson, and L. Vincent.

On April 3, 1948, a tragedy occurred on the Delaware River, south of New Castle, Delaware, when a rowboat capsized and four young people drowned. Having assisted firefighters, the Delaware State Police realized there was a need within the department for a water rescue vehicle. Shortly after, the Delaware State Police purchased an inboard powerboat and outfitted it with radios and water rescue materials. The new boat was made part of the mobile emergency field unit, which had recently been renovated.

Constantly striving for innovation, the Delaware State Police wished to extend the capability of their water force. With the large amount of waterways running around and through the state, Col. Harry Shew directed Lt. William Short, a former navy diver, to informally train a few troopers in underwater diving techniques in 1952. Pictured are Lieutenant Short (left), Trooper First Class Charles Dolan, and Trooper First Class James Turner Jr. (in water) at Lake Como in Smyrna, Delaware.

The Delaware State Police formed its first formal underwater diving unit (SCUBA) in August 1970. Initially, five troopers were sent to the Washington Navy Yard for a four-week course at the U.S. Navy Diving and Salvage School. Photographed above are four of the five original divers in the water on a training mission. They are, from left to right, G. Lake, M. Capodanno, A. Santoro, and J. Weller (J. Dickson is not shown). The demand for diver operations soon increased, and additional divers were added during the years. One of the units is shown in the late 1970s. Photographed below are, from left to right, (first row) R. Santobianco, G. Lake, D. Marvel, and W. Griffith; (second row) J. Weller, J. Hitchens, R. Harms, and J. Dickson. The uniform officer standing far right is unidentified.

As with most techniques involving specialization, there is usually a historical precedent that can be found, and special weapons teams are a case in point. In the early years of the Delaware State Police, special operations consisted of grabbing a "Tommy Gun" to give added firepower when confronting a foe. This training photograph from the late 1930s or possibly the early 1940s demonstrates this technique.

As with all things evolutionary, Special Operations Response Units, sometimes known as SWAT, have evolved into highly trained, cohesive units that are tasked with a number of functions. These include hostage negotiations, warrant executions, and protective details. Consisting of numerous members, they are highly trained and extremely well-qualified marksman. As a member of this elite unit, Trooper Charles McCall is shown clothed in a ghillie suit.

Public relations is an often-overlooked function of the Delaware State Police in its ongoing role of protecting the citizens of the state of Delaware. An early priority of the state police was educating the general public as to the latest crime-fighting technology. In the 1940s, this was accomplished by interacting with the public at the Kent-Sussex Fair, which has evolved into the Delaware State Fair.

Another function of the Delaware State Police is child safety, which entails the education of parents and their children to be aware of the latest tactics used by child predators. Capt. Robert Regan demonstrates a technique used to entice young children to go with a stranger during an interactive campaign around 1959. Educating the children of our citizens continues to be a priority of the Delaware State Police, along with the restructuring of laws regarding this issue.

Seven

Civilian Support Unit

When the Delaware State Police was established, little thought was given to the infrastructure needed to assist officers. Beyond mechanics for motorcycle repairs, ancillary clerical tasks were ignored. As the state police grew, initially, men were hired to perform this function. World War II changed this, and three females, Rena DiDonato, Mary Givens, and Myrtle Fahs were hired to process clerical work, and thus began what is known today as the Civilian Support Unit.

A number of Delaware State Police officers were veterans of World War I and reenlisted in the military, while others felt a desire to protect our country rather than just the state of Delaware. As the country entered its second year of the war, and in order to offset the shortage of manpower, seven young women were hired by the state police during 1943 to assist with clerical duties. Rena DiDonato transferred to the state highway department, which left two ladies from 1942 to be supplemented by the seven newly hired females. Pictured above are the original nine females listed from left to right: (first row) Laura McElwee, Mary Haines, Mary Draper, and Florence Stafford; (second row) Naomi Hughes, Myrtle Fahs, Frances Downey, Verona Smith, and Betty Givens Eldridge. Pictured below is Verona Lee Smith and the identification card issued during her time of employment.

DELAWARE STATE POLICE

(Department)

Name Verona Lee Smith

Date of Birth Oct.24, 1922

Position Stenopgrapher Station # 5

Date Appointed 9-14-43

REMARKS

resigned 3-15-44

Described as clerical workers in some publications, the first females served a far greater function during their employment with the Delaware State Police. While some filing was done, these ladies were tasked as telephone operators, receptionists, secretaries, stenographers, and radio operators. Their role within the Delaware State Police was multifunctional and indeed an asset to the department's ability to continue to function during trying times. Naomi Hughes (above) is shown at Station No. 1, Penny Hill, serving as a receptionist and radio operator. Mary Draper (below) is performing her duties at the Bureau of Identification, Station No. 2, headquarters.

As employees of the Delaware State Police, civilian females wore a distinctive uniform. The uniform consisted of a jacket, skirt, and pointed hat, all khaki colored with blue piping and a badge. Their blouse was white with the second "hen and chicks" patch on the left shoulder. Hired initially for the war years, women civilian employees have since played an increasingly important role in providing support services for the uniformed members of the Delaware State Police. Pictured above is Mary Draper operating the headquarters switchboard at Station No. 2. Frances Downey (at left) is shown doing an identification search at the Bureau of Identification, headquarters, Station No. 2.

As the Delaware State Police moved forward into the 1950s, the Civilian Support Unit began to develop and grow with the hiring of additional personnel. Civilians moved into areas beyond their initial function as the department increased in size and scope. In 1958, the unit had grown well beyond the original nine ladies of 1943. As the new headquarters at Dover was completed in May of that year, the ladies shown above from left to right—(first row) Mary Karkos, Lois Deputy, Ruth Ann McVey, Anne Hutson, and Margaret Welch; (second row) Betty Bennett, Delma Price, Pat Jackson, Evelyn Covelli, and Winifred O'Neill—were responsible for moving the Delaware State Police Headquarters from State Road to Dover. Also in the 1950s, secretaries were added to the complement of employees at each of the troops. Pictured below is Connie Dick at Troop 4, Georgetown. Connie is the longest-serving member of the Delaware State Police.

The Civilian Support Unit has expanded beyond its original intent, which was to serve as a stopgap measure during the war years. Civilians, as the years have passed, can be found in the Traffic Section, the Criminal Section, the State Bureau of Identification, and secretarial and clerical positions at headquarters and each of the troops. Mary Karkos (above) is well remembered from her headquarters days and also as a sometimes-cantankerous receptionist at Troop 2, State Road. Pictured below are Harry Ledoum (farthest right), Marie Kisner (center), and Frances Majerus at headquarters, Traffic Section.

Due to the nature of the work with the Delaware State Police, many civilians have come and gone from the workforce. Some, however, have made the department their home and, for that reason, will always be remembered. Five of these employees are pictured above on their 20th anniversary with the Delaware State Police. They are, from left to right, Elizabeth Foster, Emma DiDonato, Delma Price, Johnny Johnson, and Connie Dick. The work can be tedious, especially in the State Bureau of Identification, and many civilians move onto other areas of employment. Pictured below are Terri Welch (left) and Connie Spicer doing data entry at the State Bureau of Identification in the 1970s.

Most individuals in the Civilian Support Unit move through their careers with the Delaware State Police largely unseen while performing their daily tasks. Many are unknown to the uniform personnel unless there is some interaction which draws them together. Bernice Biddle (above) and Elisa Vassas (below) are exceptions to the rule. Mrs. Biddle began her employment at headquarters in 1958 and has served as a secretary and executive secretary for nine colonels of the Delaware State Police. She retired in 1994. Elisa Vassas, the state police photographer, came to the Delaware State Police in 1980. She is charged with the responsibility of maintaining the photographic files of the division, photographing personnel and special events, and offering photographic expertise to both the Traffic and Criminal Divisions. Ms. Vassas is shown here assisting the Delaware State Police SCUBA team on one of their missions.

Two other females who were well known during their employment with the Delaware State Police took different courses in their careers. Janet Vetter (at right) served in both the State Bureau of Identification and the Traffic Section from 1979 until her untimely death. She was a well-known figure within the Delaware State Police civilian community. Mary Kessel (below) came to the state police in 1971. Her first job was hand-coding criminal reports. The Delaware State Police was the first law enforcement agency in the state to receive computers to enter criminal reports. When other agencies began getting computers, she and a partner trained every police department in the state to enter criminal reports via the computer. Mrs. Kessel left the position in 1980 and transferred to another area within the state government.

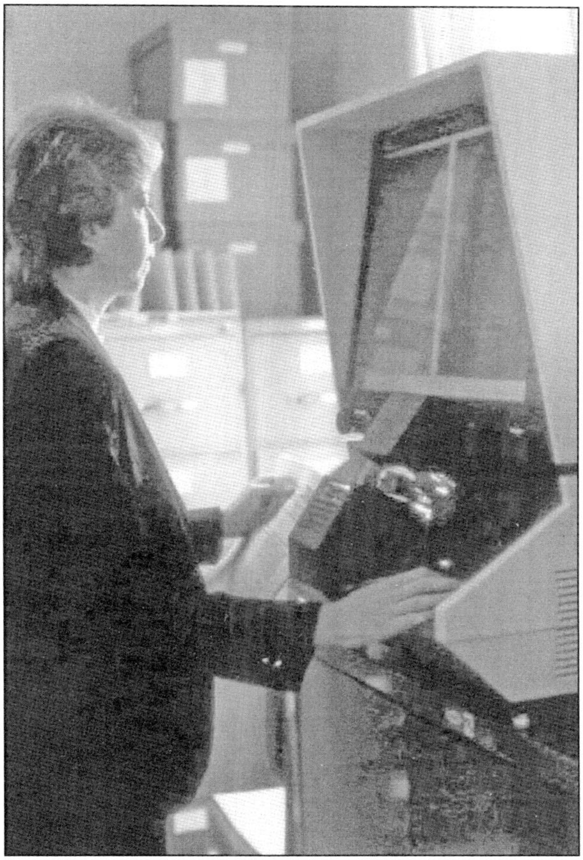

The Civilian Support Unit of the Delaware State Police has grown dramatically from its beginnings with just a few men and women in the 1930s and 1940s. To help put it in perspective, the photograph above shows the headquarters clerical staff around 1973. It has grown dramatically from the nine females hired in 1943 to 17. The photograph below of the State Bureau of Identification around 1980 is a far cry from the one-man Bureau of Identification established in 1935 by Sgt. William Knecht at Station No. 1, Penny Hill.

Eight

The Museum

The Delaware State Police Museum is dedicated to the history of the department. Several active and retired individuals had a vision in the early 1990s to establish a center to house the department's artifacts. The state police is proud of its heritage and wants to share it with the public. From humble beginnings, see the evolution of one of the foremost and modern law enforcement agencies in the United States.

Visitors from far and wide, national and international, have visited Delaware to take a walk through the history of the Delaware State Police at the museum. Upon entering the museum, guests are first requested to share in a somber moment as they pass a large black granite wall upon which are the photographs of the 22 brave men and women who made the ultimate sacrifice to protect the citizens of Delaware. The entrance to the museum (above) is on the south side of the main hall. After entering the building, visitors turn right (below) and pass the flag-draped memorial wall.

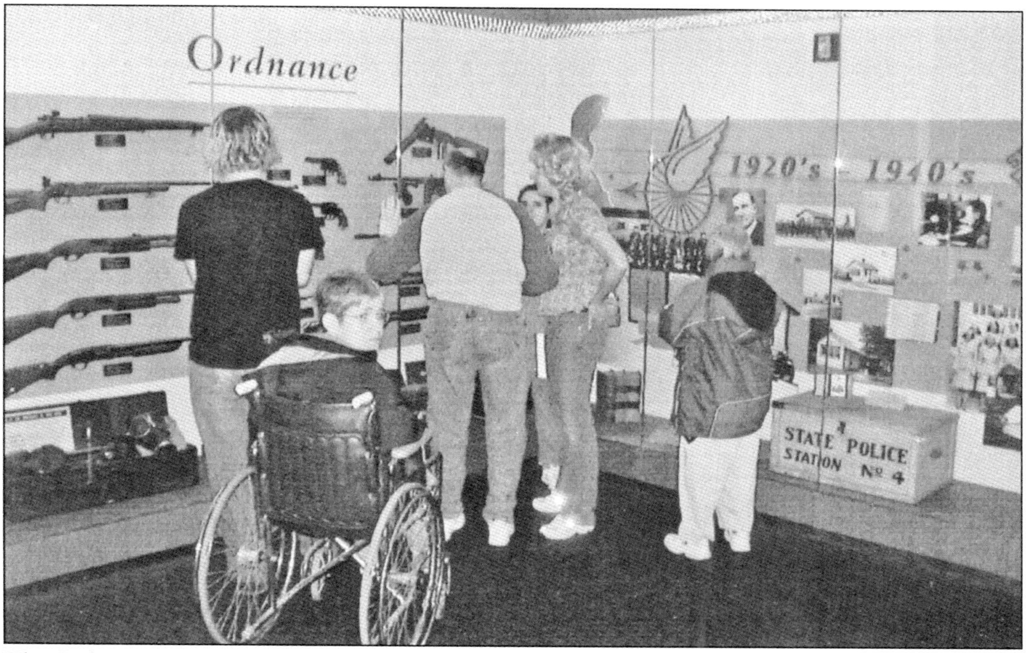

The Delaware State Police Museum, in addition to being a repository for the Delaware State Police history, is an educational facility where safety education, DARE (Drug Abuse Assistance Education), and other programs are presented in a classroom and auditorium. Instructors within the Delaware State Police can be scheduled to present classes on a variety of topics. Guided tours are also available for groups by appointment. A special needs group (above) and the attendees at Troop Youth Week (below) show the diverse use of the museum.

Delaware, the First State, has provided innovation through the years, and the Delaware State Police Museum and Educational Center carries on this rich tradition. Groups of all ages have been welcomed to the museum. The museum is particularly proud of its commitment to preschool children and also to various gifted children and gifted adult groups. The picture above is a gifted adult group, and the smiles on their faces speak volumes. The poster below was assembled by a group of preschoolers and is a touching reminder of their appreciation. It is displayed along with the other cherished artifacts at the museum.

The museum is a historical panorama of times past through the near present. Visitors can view replicas of three original patrol vehicles as well as motorcycles that were used to patrol the roadways of Delaware. Amateur investigators are also welcome to attempt to solve a mock murder or revisit a real crime scene in miniature (above). A replica of old Troop 4 allows visitors a glimpse of policing in the 1920s and Trooper Dan, the first talking car, allows many to relive their youth (below). The exhibits and hands-on displays are truly an adventure for those who like to wander. If you have a friend or relative who is retired from the Delaware State Police, visit "Roll Call" and renew your relationship.

One of the latest projects undertaken by the Delaware State Police Museum was the acquisition of a replica of the first Delaware State Police helicopter. With the assistance of the Delaware State Police Aviation Unit, which worked directly with the U.S. Air Force at Dover, a military version of the Bell 206 Jet Ranger was acquired in 2008. Through museum funding and donations, the OH-58 Kiowa helicopter (above) was restored. It was placed on a pedestal (below) for visitors to view. This helicopter, known affectionately as "HQ 501," served the citizens of Delaware as a medevac from 1971 to 1975. The museum restored the exterior of the helicopter, and it has been painted in its original colors.

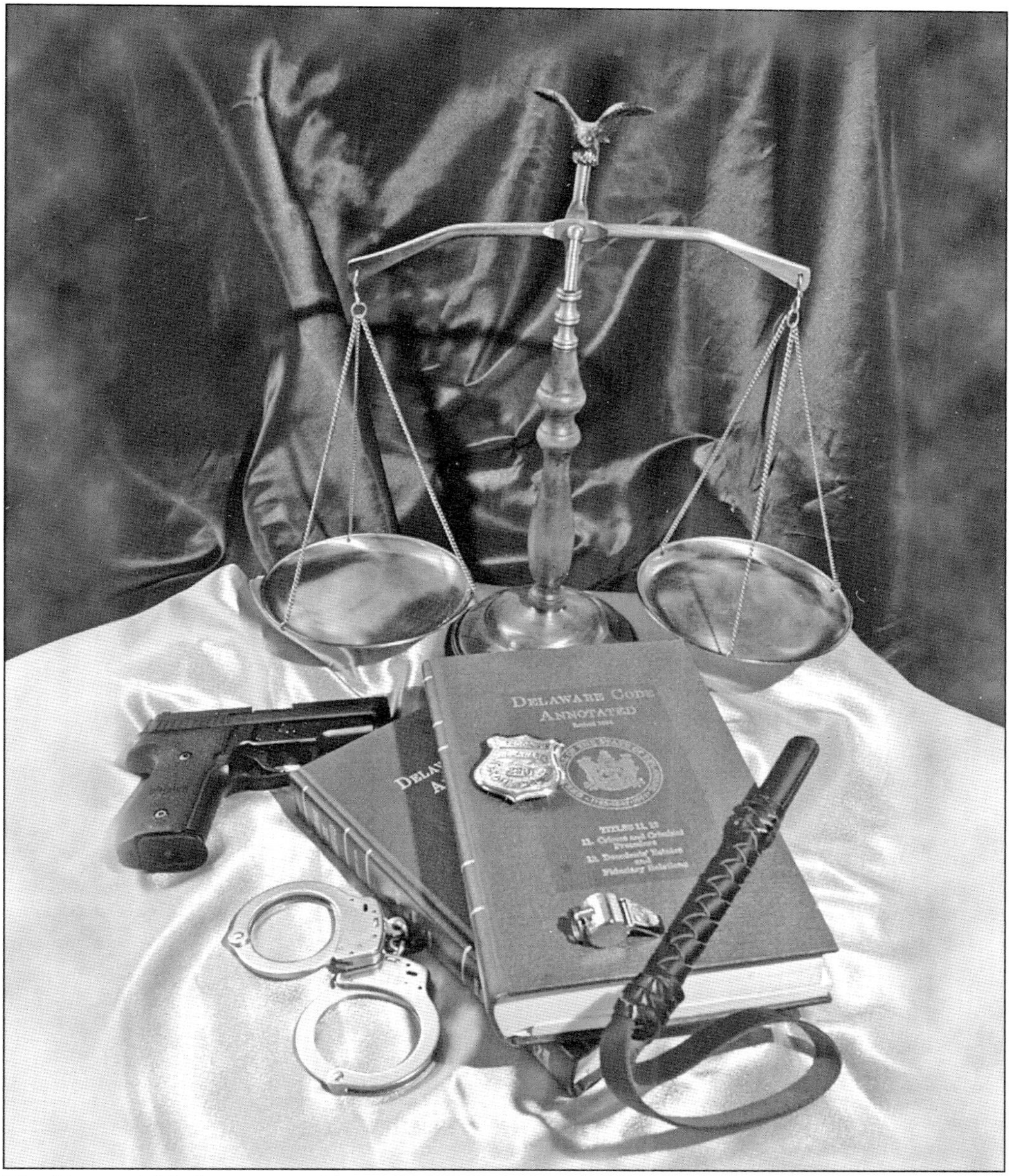

The Trooper's Pledge is recited by each new trooper as he begins his service as a member of the Delaware State Police: "Humbly recognizing the responsibilities entrusted to me as a member of the Department of State Police, an organization dedicated to the preservation of property and human life. I pledge myself to perform my duties honestly and faithfully to the best of my ability without, fear, favor, or prejudice. I shall aid those in danger or distress, and shall strive always to make my State and Country a safer place in which to live. I shall wage unceasing war against crime in all its forms, and shall consider no sacrifice to great in the performance of my duty. I shall obey the laws of the United States of America . . . and the State of Delaware . . . and shall support and defend their constitutions against all enemies whomsoever, foreign or domestic. I shall always be loyal to and uphold the honor of my organization, my State, and my Country." (Courtesy of Elisa A. Vassas.)

www.arcadiapublishing.com

Discover books about the town where you grew up, the cities where your friends and families live, the town where your parents met, or even that retirement spot you've been dreaming about. Our Web site provides history lovers with exclusive deals, advanced notification about new titles, e-mail alerts of author events, and much more.

MADE IN THE USA

Arcadia Publishing, the leading local history publisher in the United States, is committed to making history accessible and meaningful through publishing books that celebrate and preserve the heritage of America's people and places. Consistent with our mission to preserve history on a local level, this book was printed in South Carolina on American-made paper and manufactured entirely in the United States.

This book carries the accredited Forest Stewardship Council (FSC) label and is printed on 100 percent FSC-certified paper. Products carrying the FSC label are independently certified to assure consumers that they come from forests that are managed to meet the social, economic, and ecological needs of present and future generations.

FSC
Mixed Sources
Product group from well-managed forests and other controlled sources

Cert no. SW-COC-001530
www.fsc.org
© 1996 Forest Stewardship Council